Rolli Snowballs

by Michael Delgado
illustrated by Mircea Catusanu

HOUGHTON MIFFLIN   BOSTON

Printed in China

ISBN 10: 0-618-88671-0
ISBN 13: 978-0-618-88671-5

15 16 17 18 19 0940 20 19 18 17 16
4500590851

The 3 bears wanted
to make a snow bear.
"Our snow bear can be
king of the hill," said Ken.

"This snowball is heavier,"
said Kelly.
"I think you and I can roll this
one up together," said Ken.

4   Which snowball is heavier?

They made 3 snowballs.
They tried to roll them up hill.
"I can roll this snowball up,"
said Pete. "It is not heavy."

Which snowball is lightest?

"This one is very heavy!" said Ken.
"Maybe if we all push, we could roll
this one," said Kelly. "Let's try!"

"We can do it," said Pete.
"Don't give up!" said Kelly.
"Push together, 1, 2, 3. Go!"
said Ken.

Why were 3 bears needed to push?

The bears made the snowballs
look like a snow bear.
"It is the king of the hill,"
said Ken.

Heavy Snowballs

Draw

Follow Directions Oral and Written **Look** at pages 4 and 5. Draw the 3 snowballs you see. Make sure they are different sizes.

Tell About

Look at page 5. Tell about the snowballs you see. Tell why 3 bears are needed to push the snowball.

Write

Look at page 5. Write why 3 bears are pushing the biggest snowball.